# YOUR KNOWLEDGE HAS VALUE

- We will publish your bachelor's and master's thesis, essays and papers

- Your own eBook and book - sold worldwide in all relevant shops

- Earn money with each sale

Upload your text at www.GRIN.com
and publish for free

**Bibliographic information published by the German National Library:**

The German National Library lists this publication in the National Bibliography; detailed bibliographic data are available on the Internet at http://dnb.dnb.de .

This book is copyright material and must not be copied, reproduced, transferred, distributed, leased, licensed or publicly performed or used in any way except as specifically permitted in writing by the publishers, as allowed under the terms and conditions under which it was purchased or as strictly permitted by applicable copyright law. Any unauthorized distribution or use of this text may be a direct infringement of the author s and publisher s rights and those responsible may be liable in law accordingly.

**Imprint:**

Copyright © 2015 GRIN Verlag
Print and binding: Books on Demand GmbH, Norderstedt Germany
ISBN: 9783668718340

**This book at GRIN:**

https://www.grin.com/document/427437

Katharina Gerhardt

# Reality and Perception of Reality in Virginia Woolf's Short Stories

GRIN Verlag

**GRIN - Your knowledge has value**

Since its foundation in 1998, GRIN has specialized in publishing academic texts by students, college teachers and other academics as e-book and printed book. The website www.grin.com is an ideal platform for presenting term papers, final papers, scientific essays, dissertations and specialist books.

**Visit us on the internet:**

http://www.grin.com/

http://www.facebook.com/grincom

http://www.twitter.com/grin_com

Johannes Gutenberg-Universität Mainz

Fachbereich 05: Philosophie und Philologie

Summer Term 2015

Proseminar: "Modernist Short Stories"

"The familiar is not necessarily the known" (G.W.F. Hegel)
Reality and Perception of Reality in
Virginia Woolf's Short Stories

Katharina Gerhardt

BA American Studies

4th Semester

# Inhaltsverzeichnis

1. Introduction..................................................................................................................3
2. Main Part....................................................................................................................4
   2.1 Constructing Reality through the Narrative........................................................4
   2.2 Who Creates the Narratives?...............................................................................6
   2.3 The End: Revelation............................................................................................8
3. Conclusion..................................................................................................................9
4. Bibliography.............................................................................................................10

# 1. Introduction

"No, no, nothing is proved, nothing is known (58)."

This quote from "The Mark on the Wall" already reveals one of the major themes of Virginia Woolf's writing, the uncertainty of knowledge. By using a unique style of writing she shows how we try to make sense of our lives and give meaning to everything in the world. At the same time there is a profound feeling of not being able to fully understand what this existence is about.

By analyzing two of her short stories, "The Mark on the Wall" and "An Unwritten Novel", I will examine Woolf's method of showing the contrast between what we think reality to be and what reality actually is. Therefore, I argue that in her short stories Virginia Woolf demonstrates how we construct realities and meanings for ourselves through creating narratives and how easily these narratives are exposed as fragile and unstable.

In the first part of my analysis, I will examine how she uses these narratives to show how we make up realities for ourselves in order to make sense of the outside world. Then, I will continue with analyzing who these constructed realities come from and how she criticizes society through this. Lastly, it will be looked at the fragility of these constructed realities and how Woolf shows that what we think we know and what something really is, are not necessarily the same. She illustrates how incomplete and vague our assumptions and perceptions can be whenever we think we have fully understood something and offers different views on knowledge and reality at the ends of her stories.

## 2. Main Part

## 2.1 Constructing Reality through the Narrative

Woolf's way of demonstrating how we construct realities for ourselves is to use narratives within the narrative itself, she creates fiction within fiction. A perfect example of this is her short story "An Unwritten Novel". In this, the narrator makes up her own tale about the female passenger who sits in the train compartment with her. The method of giving the reader an insight into the narrator's mind (stream of consciousness), creates different layers to the story and illustrates our tendency as human beings to always make assumptions about other people's lives and the world around us. The narrator believes to have understood the woman's "message" and "deciphered her secret, reading it beneath her gaze" (27). Through this separate narrative Virginia Woolf shows how we make up our own truths about the meaning of things in our minds in order to at least try and make sense of ourselves and the things and people around us.

> In reference to the opposition of subjective and objective thought, the novels on one hand express and on the other formulate the perpetual tension between the world in consciousness and the world in reality. (Love 77)

This quote demonstrates how Woolf exposes the contrast between the world in our mind and the real world in her writings. Nóra Séllei also mentions how in "An Unwritten Novel" the narrative "I" imagines a truth and tries to decode and "contextualise [the other woman] socially, economically, psychologically, and emotionally" (192).

The construction of reality is obvious in the narrator's behavior towards the other passenger, as she draws conclusions from and interprets the woman's actions, although she does not even know this person's background, she just simply starts making it up. This means that we always need to see something more in others, we project our own experiences onto them and reflect their actions as with "the speck on the glass" (27). The narrator is basically reading things into the other woman when thinking: "Oh, she committed some crime!" and continues to wrap an entire fictive story around this person who she actually does not know anything about (29). "Have I read you right?" the narrator asks the other woman in her thoughts, secretly knowing that she is only talking to herself, that she will not get an answer, because her "reality" is really only in her mind and the true reality might never be fully accessible to her. Once she thinks to have found it, it shifts again, "I wish I could piece them [fragments] together! If you would only sit still" (30-31). The imagined character of the narrative becomes even clearer when the narrator starts making up more and more characters and background stories as if writing a novel (32). Phillips mentions that Woolf's method shows that our "knowledge" is actually very subjective by demonstrating that experience always depends on the individual's perception of something and the question remains, whether there is any objective knowledge we can really gain (424).

The same can be seen in "The Mark on the Wall" in which the plot basically consists of the narrator making assumptions on what the mysterious mark could be, while getting distracted by other thoughts. In this story, the narrator seems to realize the contrast already mentioned above and her own inability to change something about it. It is implied that we can only ever see fragments of other people's lives when we rush past in the train and she compares life to "being blown through the Tube..." and remarks "how very little control of our possessions we have" (54). Hussey points out that Woolf always goes back and forth between believing that there is meaning and sense in the world and the notion that life is absurd and unpredictable (96). So on the one hand we sometimes get small pieces of truth and we try hard to find more and on the other hand it seems in vain to look for more truth, because we will only ever scratch the surface.

The narrator mentions how we are "groping at the roots of the grass", saying that she really wants to find something that goes deeper than the surface "with its hard separate facts" (54-55). She wants to find some "pleasant thought" about herself and realizes that we also construct how we want to see ourselves in our mind, while others only see the outside. This again describes the contrast between perception and reality, since we can never truly see the person as a whole when we look at someone, we can only see what we believe to be real (56). Lazenby describes how the narrator is aware of possible misinterpretations of herself by others and knows that we can make wrong assumptions about others and the things around us, therefore she tries to protect her image of herself (111).

Ultimately, it can be said that Virginia Woolf recognized where we fail to go beyond the surface and what is commonly accepted as real. She demonstrates the desire of humanity to find a deeper meaning and gain objective knowledge. In order to do that we tend to create our own fictional stories around, for instance, another person, while forgetting that it is just in our mind and that we judge and interpret this person simply based on our subjective perceptions and experiences, which are influenced by various factors and therefore unstable, leading to us being unable to get a definite understanding of the world. In the next chapter I will deal with the reasons for and creators of the constructed realities.

## 2.2 Who Creates the Narratives?

As human beings we have certain ways of creating a reality for ourselves. This construction of reality is influenced by several factors. Woolf mainly points out society with its norms, standards and facts as influences on our understanding of things: "The world we see is subject to our mental states, but our mental states are subject to the crowded, fantastic, and unpredictable outside world" (Phillips 418). This means that everything we perceive underlies the rules of our mind, but also our way of perceiving is influenced by external elements.

In "The Mark on the Wall" the narrator mentions "[t]here was a rule for everything" and continues that she discovered "that these real things, Sunday luncheons, Sunday walks, […] were not entirely real, were indeed half phantoms […]" (57). Woolf shows how we, as human beings, need rules for everything and always have to name, categorize and generalize it all. There are books and newspapers on all topics giving us suggestions on what to believe in, so here we can see how the narrator becomes conscious of our need for rituals and the imagined truth in these supposedly real things. Caughie talks about this quality of Woolf's writing when she says that "reality is itself a construct, a plurality of stories others have created" (39).

Woolf tries to show that our understanding of knowledge is what we know from certain books or that we accept things to be true that have the reputation of being true, but she tries to show that this is not real knowledge, these standard conceptions of reality established by media and "learned men" cannot claim the ultimate truth for themselves. Society might teach us to believe in these generalized facts it has set up to be reality, but as Woolf demonstrates through her writing, these "truths" are fragile and can easily be questioned depending on the viewpoint of a particular person (57). She criticizes the individual for not questioning these "truths" advocated in *The Times* or "Whitaker's Table of Precedency", and for just believing in them. This is "the masculine point of view which governs our lives, which sets the standard", the narrator realizes and these man-made "truths" should be replaced just like all the other things thought to be true and real before (57).

So the narrative power lies in the big and popular names, for example, newspapers or certain influential books and other things which are valued and believed in by the general public and hardly ever questioned. We are influenced by these views and therefore also create our own "realities" around this way of thinking, because it is easier to believe in and invent a truth behind something than to try and find the true meaning and sense of life and the world for oneself. For this matter, the narrator of "A Mark on the Wall" explains how humanity actually did not make much progress when it comes to having real knowledge, people are still caught up in their superstitions, still do not think for themselves and are guided by the rules and norms formed by a specific part of society, namely mostly by men in a certain, higher position. If we made ourselves free of this man-made "truth" that is really only speculation, we could live in a much more peaceful and pleasant world (58). As Sim points out, the story "encourages a mental movement away from a world of common-sense 'surface' facts and the natural attitude, which are associated with male intellectual authority and social convention…" (45).

The same can be observed in "An Unwritten Novel" in which *The Times* is presented as a source of knowledge: "…it's all in *The Times*" (26). Woolf wants to show how we are influenced in our perception by what we are told by these supposed sources of knowledge. The newspaper "functions as a symbol of self-evident conclusions, of ready-made truth, of facts served daily as life, as a repository of the essence of existence" (Séllei 193). It presents us with meanings which we can build around the things we perceive and makes it easier for us to create our own characters and realities, regardless of the real "truth" in them.

Woolf demonstrates how we try to find reality in the visible, only in what we can perceive, something we can experience with our senses, but as Hussey explains Woolf wanted to "express perception of a 'reality' that transcends all modalities and gives them their being" (97). He continues to say that her reality was one that went "behind and beyond actual life" (151).

In the two short stories this notion of man-made truths made up by us as human beings in order to get answers for everything forms the contrast to what Woolf considered "reality". We want to go beyond the surface and find something behind the visible world, but still always stay within the limits of our perception and make ourselves dependent on them. We try to ignore our lack of real knowledge, because as Woolf shows, knowledge is not what "learned" men and the media popularize, but something independent of sensual perception.

## 2.3 The End: Revelation

At the end of the short stories, both narrators have a revelation. In "The Mark on the Wall" what the narrator thought to be real and true was not so true after all. All the assumptions made about the snail and making it into something more important than it really was, were really unnecessary. Fleishman describes how undetermined and speculative our thoughts on a perceived object can be and how our realities are layered and shifting from one to the other (53-54). He also speaks about the sense of a profound uncertainty and that the two stories basically deal with the same topic: "moving from what seems to be easily grasped to what is tenuous and ultimately unknowable- even though it seems to be controlled when a name is assigned" (69).

At the end of "An Unwritten Novel" the narrator is left shocked at the exposure of her constructed reality and her ignorance of the truth, she does not want to believe she really did not gain any real knowledge. Therefore the end creates a feeling of losing one's ground, nothing seems real anymore. But still the narrator does not stop asking questions, she is still convinced that there is something more, and is still curious about the "mysterious figures" and "adorable world" (36). This leaves the impression in the reader that maybe there could be something more underneath, but that we might not be able to ever succeed in finding the core of everything with our limited ability to acquire knowledge.

In "The Mark on the Wall" the topic of the uncertainty of knowledge is the same, but the end suggests that maybe the "real" knowledge we seek, is actually something very simple and not as important as we believe it to be and that civilization did not hold the ultimate answer or acquire any essential knowledge (60).

Woolf wants to get past this, beyond the shell, behind the visible and tangible world and what is generally believed to be reality. Ultimately, it seems like this is what art was about for Woolf. She gives different perspectives and looks through the body and the surface in order to find something more lasting and permanent and to expose to the reader the fragility and instability of the "realities" we create for ourselves just to make sense of our lives. Art and life complement one another and art can enable us to overcome the barriers of perception and give us different perspectives on life and the world just like Woolf does by holding up the mirror to society and suggesting different ways of looking at life, revealing our attempt to hide our own ignorance and lack of "real" knowledge.

## 3. Conclusion

Woolf demonstrates that our realities are layered since we all create different meanings for ourselves in order to make sense of our lives. At the same time she suggests that maybe all our trying to find a deeper truth is in vain, because we will not ever be able to fully grasp it. Another suggestion is that we struggle to find out what is behind something, but in the end it turns out to be something very simple, something rather meaningless on the outside, which we still might not ever be able to decode with our common way of seeking knowledge.

Ultimately, both stories deal with how we construct knowledge for ourselves through inventing our own stories about other people or other things and our own existence. What we keep forgetting though is that these assumptions are only in our minds and created through our perceptions, which are influenced by society's continuously changing norms and trends as well as our obsession with categorizing and naming everything. We are shocked when we are torn from our changing and fragmentary reality and try to compensate for our lack of real knowledge. Woolf motivates readers to get a different perspective on reality other than what our senses and beliefs imply, because they are limited and often unreliable.

# 4. Bibliography

Caughie, Pamela L. *Virginia Woolf & Postmodernism- Literature in Quest & Question of Itself.* Urbana: University of Illinois Press, 1991. Print.

Fleishman, Avrom. "Forms of the Woolfian Short Story". *Virginia Woolf- Revaluation and Continuity.* Ed. Ralph Freedman. Berkely: University of California Press, 1980. 44-70. Print.

Hussey, Mark. *The Singing of the Real World-The Philosophy of Virginia Woolf's Fiction.* Columbus: Ohio State University Press, 1986. Print.

Lazenby, Donna J. *A Mystical Philosophy- Transcendence and Immanence in the Works of Virginia Woolf and Iris Murdoch.* London: Bloomsbury, 2014. Print.

Love, Jean O., *Worlds in Consciousness- Mythopoetic Thought in the Novels Of Virginia Woolf.* Berkeley: University of California Press, 1970. Print.

Phillips, Brian. "Reality and Virginia Woolf". *The Hudson Review* 56.3 (2003):415-430. Web. 15 Aug. 2015. <http://www.jstor.org/stable/3852679>.

Séllei, Nóra. "The Snail and *The Times*: Three Stories 'Dancing in Unity'". *Hungarian Journal of English and American Studies* 3.2 (1997): 189-198. Web. 15 Aug. 2015. <http://www.jstor.org/stable/41273965>.

Sim, Lorraine. *Virginia Woolf: The Patterns of Ordinary Experience.* Farnham: Ashgate Publishing, 2010. Print.

Woolf, Virginia. *Selected Short Stories.* Ed. Sandra Kemp. London: Penguin Books, 1993. Print.

# YOUR KNOWLEDGE HAS VALUE

- We will publish your bachelor's and master's thesis, essays and papers

- Your own eBook and book - sold worldwide in all relevant shops

- Earn money with each sale

Upload your text at www.GRIN.com and publish for free